Contents

Safety note:
Ask an adult to help you with
the activities in this book.

What is a pumpkin?

A pumpkin is the **fruit** of the pumpkin plant. It is usually orange, but it can also be red, yellow, or white. Inside is the flesh, and also the **seeds**.

A big, round pumpkin is heavy to hold!

FIFE COUNCIL LIBRARIES

FB110494

Gr...w ...self!

...ur Own

...P

Please return or renew this item before the latest date shown below

Renewals can be made
by internet   www.fifedirect.org.uk/libraries
in person   at any library in Fife
by phone   08451 55 00 66

Fife

Thank you for using your library

www.raintreepublishers.co.uk
Visit our website to find out
more information about
Raintree books.

To order:
☎ Phone 0845 6044371
📄 Fax +44 (0) 1865 312263
✉ Email myorders@raintreepublishers.co.uk

Customers from outside the UK please telephone +44 1865 312262

Raintree is an imprint of Capstone Global Library Limited,
a company incorporated in England and Wales having its
registered office at 7 Pilgrim Street, London, EC4V 6LB
– Registered company number: 6695582

Text © Capstone Global Library Limited 2012
First published in hardback in 2012
First published in paperback in 2013
The moral rights of the proprietor have been asserted.

Edited by Daniel Nunn, Rebecca Rissman, and Sian Smith
Designed by Philippa Jenkins
Picture research by Mica Brancic
Production by Victoria Fitzgerald
Originated by Capstone Global Library Ltd
Printed and bound in China by Leo Paper Products Ltd

ISBN 978 1 406 22476 4 (hardback)
15 14 13 12 11
10 9 8 7 6 5 4 3 2 1

ISBN 978 1 406 22483 2 (paperback)
16 15 14 13 12
10 9 8 7 6 5 4 3 2 1

British Library Cataloguing in Publication Data
Malam, John, 1957-
   Grow your own soup. -- (Grow it yourself!)
   1. Vegetable gardening--Juvenile literature. 2. Soups--
Juvenile literature.
   I. Title II. Series
   635-dc22

Acknowledgements
The author and publisher are grateful to the following for
permission to reproduce copyright material: Alamy p. 18
(© Alison Thompson); © Capstone Publishers pp. 13, 15, 21,
26, 27, 28, 29 bottom, 29 top (Karon Dubke); Corbis p. 6
(© Robert Galbraith/Reuters); GAP Photos pp. 9 (Christine
Bollen), 11 (Maxine Adcock), 20 (Zara Napier); iStockphoto
p. 23 (© Rich Legg); © John Malam pp. 24, 25; Photolibrary
pp. 4 (Garden Picture Library/Stephen Shepherd), 8 (Garden
Picture Library/Mark Bolton), 14 (Garden Picture Library/
Francesca Yorke); Shutterstock pp. 5 (© Marilyn Volan), 7
(© Stephen Coburn), 10, 17, 19 (© Denis and Yulia
Pogostins), 12 (© Losevsky Pavel), 16 (© Saiko3p), 22
(© Tatagatta).

Background cover photograph of pumpkins in a Thanksgiving
fair reproduced with permission of Shutterstock (© Ckchiu).
Foreground cover photograph of a bowl of pumpkin soup
reproduced with permission of © Capstone Publishers
(Karon Dubke)

Every effort has been made to contact copyright holders
of material reproduced in this book. Any omissions will
be rectified in subsequent printings if notice is given to the
publisher.

To find out about the author, visit his website:
www.johnmalam.co.uk

Some words are shown in bold, **like this**. You can
find out what they mean by looking in the glossary.

Farmers grow long rows of pumpkins in fields.

A few weeks after pumpkin **seeds** have been **sown**, the plants make flowers. After a few days, baby pumpkins appear. When they are **ripe**, they are ready to pick. Pumpkins are a healthy food.

Big and small

There are many types of pumpkin **fruit**. Some are mini pumpkins, the size of oranges. Other pumpkins become giant sizes. The biggest pumpkins are the heaviest fruits in the world.

There are competitions to grow giant pumpkins, like these.

Some pumpkins are small.

Each type of pumpkin has a name. Jack-Be-Little is the name of a mini pumpkin. Atlantic Giant is the name of a monster-sized pumpkin. Pumpkin names can be funny, such as Red Warty Thing!

Creepers and climbers

Pumpkin plants grow by creeping along the ground, or by climbing up frames. Big pumpkins grow on creeping plants because of their size and weight.

Pumpkin plants spread or creep across the ground before they make their fruit.

mini pumpkin

frame

Mini pumpkins are much smaller and lighter than their bigger cousins. Mini pumpkins can be grown to climb up frames.

Where to grow

Pumpkin plants are grown outside on open ground. They grow into very big plants. They need a lot of space to spread out, especially if they are the type that creep along the ground.

This pumpkin plant is gradually creeping across the soil.

Pumpkins will grow over the sides of large pots like this.

The plants like to grow in a sunny spot in a garden border or a vegetable patch. They can also be grown in large pots or **planters** – but they still need a lot of space to **ramble** across.

Get ready to grow!

Garden centres have everything you need for growing pumpkin plants. Some shops and supermarkets also sell the same equipment.

There are many different types of pumpkin seeds to choose from.

To grow your own pumpkin plants you will need a packet of pumpkin **seeds**. Choose a creeping type that produces good-sized orange **fruit**, such as Howden.

You will also need: seed **compost**, medium plant pots (about 12 centimetres wide), labels, liquid plant feed, and a watering can with a **watering rose**.

Sowing the seeds

1. In April, fill the plant pots with **seed compost**.
2. Gently push the pumpkin seeds about 5 centimetres into the compost. **Sow** one seed in each pot.

Pumpkin seeds are big and easy to hold.

3. Push the seeds in edge first, not flat. This is to stop them from **rotting** if they are given too much water.

4. Sprinkle on enough compost to cover the seeds, and then label the pots.

5. Water the pots, then put them in a warm place inside. Don't let the compost dry out!

Successful seedlings

For the pumpkin **seeds** to grow, they need warmth and water. Keep the **compost moist**, but do not over water it or the seeds will **rot** away. After about fourteen days, the pumpkin plants will start to appear.

The first two leaves are called "seed leaves".

At first, the plants have two **seed leaves**. These are soon followed by **true leaves**. The **seedlings** will grow fast, pushing up through the compost and making lots of large leaves. Keep watering them.

17

Planting out

By June, the plants will be quite big. Get them used to living outside. Put them outside in the day, then bring them inside at night.

baby pumpkin plant

Dig a hole for the pumpkin plant. Put **compost** in the bottom of the hole to feed the plant.

Remove the plants from their pots. Put them into holes in the ground.

After a few days they will be ready to **plant out** into the ground. You will only need to plant one or two. Give them a drink of water.

Watering and feeding

Ask an adult to cut the bottom off a plastic drinks bottle. Then push the neck into the soil near the plant. When you pour water into it, it will go deep into the soil near the **roots**.

Pumpkin plants drink a lot of water.

Instructions on the liquid plant feed will tell you how much to use.

Pumpkin plants are hungry. Once a week, give them a feed. Mix a liquid plant feed into their water. It contains all the **nutrients** they will need.

21

Don't forget the weeding!

Weeds can be a problem, especially while the pumpkin plants are young and still quite small. Weeds take water in the soil away from the pumpkin plants.

Remove as many weeds as you can. ▼

Pumpkin plants will grow well in this weed-free patch.

Pull weeds out, or dig them up with a **hand trowel** or **hand fork**. You could cut through them with a **Dutch hoe**. Be careful not to damage the pumpkin plants.

From flower to fruit

In July, large yellow flowers appear. Some are at the end of long, thin stalks. These are male flowers. Some have short stalks and a swollen part at the end, near the **stem**. These are female flowers.

swelling

short stalk

female flower

The swelling at the end of this female flower is the start of a pumpkin.

The flowers make **pollen** which bees take from flower to flower. Baby pumpkins appear at the ends of the female flowers and begin to grow. Soon the pumpkins change colour from green to orange and are ready to pick.

Make pumpkin soup

Ask an adult to help you with the cutting and cooking.
You will need:
1 large pumpkin, 2 large onions, 4 cloves of garlic, water, milk, salt, and pepper.

1. Cut the pumpkin in half.
2. Remove the **seeds** and stringy parts.
   Peel the skin off.

3. Cut the pumpkin into small chunks.
4. Peel and chop the onions and garlic.
5. Put the pumpkin chunks, onion, and garlic into a large pot. Add water until they are almost covered.
6. Bring to the boil, then cook gently until the pumpkin is soft.

7. Remove the pot from the heat and leave it to cool.

8. Use a hand blender to blend everything together until it is smooth. It will be quite thick.

Roasted pumpkin seeds

Pumpkin **seeds** also make a tasty snack. Wash the seeds and spread them out on a baking tray. Place in a hot oven for about 30 minutes. Sprinkle with salt, then serve.

9. To serve, return to the heat and stir in some milk, or milk and water. This will thin the soup down. Add salt and pepper to taste.

Glossary

compost loose, earthy material used for growing seeds and plants

Dutch hoe a gardening tool with a flat blade and a long wooden handle

fruit the part of a plant which can often be eaten as food. Fruit contains seeds.

hand fork a small gardening tool with three pointed prongs

hand trowel a gardening tool similar to a small spade with a curved edge

moist when soil is damp but not too wet

nutrients substances that help to keep plants healthy

plant out when a plant is put into its final growing place

planter large container used for growing a plant in

pollen tiny powdery grains made by flowers

ramble when a plant crawls or creeps across the ground

ripe fully grown and ready to pick or eat

root the part of a plant that holds it in the ground. Roots collect water for the plant.

rot when a plant starts to go bad

seed the part of a plant that grows into a new plant

seed leaves the first two simple leaves of a plant

seedling a baby plant

sow to plant a seed

sown to have planted a seed

stem the main branch or trunk of a plant

true leaves all the leaves that come after the seed leaves

watering rose a sprinkler on the end of a watering can

Find out more

Books to read

Grow It, Eat It (Dorling Kindersley, 2008)

Ready, Steady, Grow!, Royal Horticultural Society (Dorling Kindersley, 2010)

Websites

www.backyardgardener.com/pumpkin.html
Look at photos of record-breaking giant pumpkins on this website and find out more about them.

www.kiddiegardens.com
This site will give you lots of ideas on how to grow plants to eat.

www.kiddiegardens.com/growing_pumpkins.html
This website is packed with advice and tips on how to grow pumpkins.

Index